I dedicate this book to my sons, AJ and Shea.
Being your mom is not just my greatest blessing, but
the very essence of my joy. With endless love—Mom

To every reader who is inspired by these
daring little dogs! I hope they encourage
you to go have grand adventures and learn
about the world around you!—E.B.

It was a bright, sunny Arizona morning. Nacho and Lola eagerly waited outside, ready to load their belongings into the RV for their upcoming trip.
"Buenos días, Nacho!" Lola said with a smile.

The Traveling Tales of Nacho & Lola

TOURING TOMBSTONE

O.K. CORRAL GUNFIGHT SITE

written by
Terrilyn M. Trejo

illustrated by
Emily Brunner

This edition first published in 2025
by Lawley Publishing,
a division of Lawley Enterprises LLC.

Hardcover ISBN 978-1-960137-8-45
Paperback ISBN 978-1-960137-86-9
Library of Congress Control Number: 2023952358

Lawley Publishing
70 S. Val Vista Dr. #A3 #188
Gilbert, AZ 85296
LawleyPublishing.com

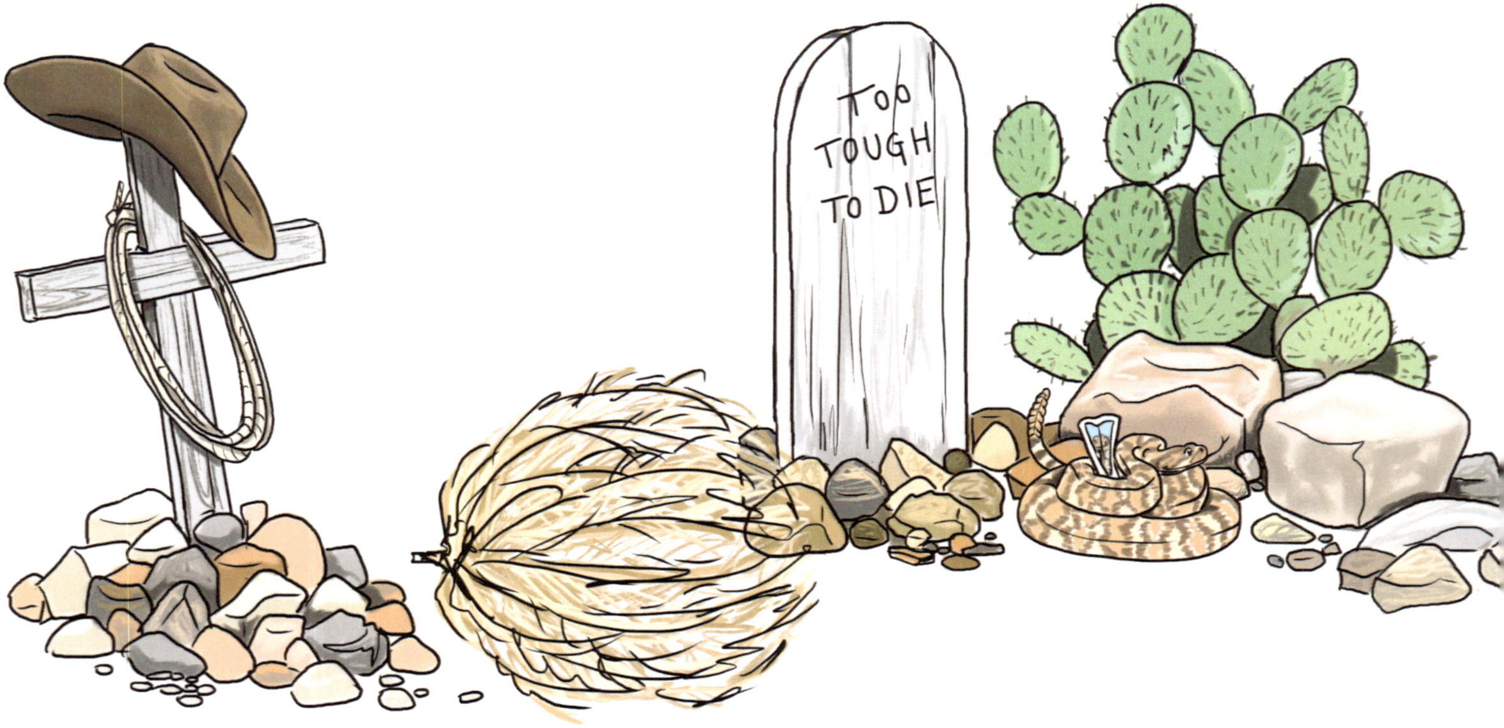

"Good morning to you, too!" Nacho wagged his tail back and forth. "I can't wait for this trip. Don't forget to pack your cowboy hat and bandana, Lola."

Suddenly, Nacho stopped and perked up his ears. "Do you hear that rattling? It sounds like our maracas," he said, looking around.

"Stop and back up slowly," Lola whispered. "That sound is coming from a rattlesnake coiled over by that rock. It's warning us to back away! We must take that warning seriously."

"Yikes!" Nacho said, moving away slowly.

The two pups carefully left the rattlesnake behind and gave a sigh of relief as they jumped into the RV. "Now," said Lola, ""back to business. Why do I need to pack my cowboy hat and bandana?"

"Because Tata Trejo says we're headed to the Wild, Wild West, to the famous town called Tombstone. I do wonder how it got that name, though, and why it's so famous," Nacho said while watching a movie on the RV television.

"I know why it's famous," Lola said proudly. "It's because of a gunfight at the O.K. Corral. And Tombstone got its name because the town's founder was told he'd only find his grave and tombstone there, not the silver or gold he was searching for."

"Yeehaw!" Nacho said wagging his tail. "That sounds like an fascinating place to visit. Let's saddle up and get this RV going."

That afternoon, the two pups rode in the RV with Tata Trejo for their short journey to Tombstone, Arizona.

When they arrived, Nacho and Lola jumped out of the RV and noticed dirt roads, old buildings, wooden boardwalks, and many people dressed in Western clothing.

"It looks like we fit right in," Lola said, straightening her bandana and cowboy hat.

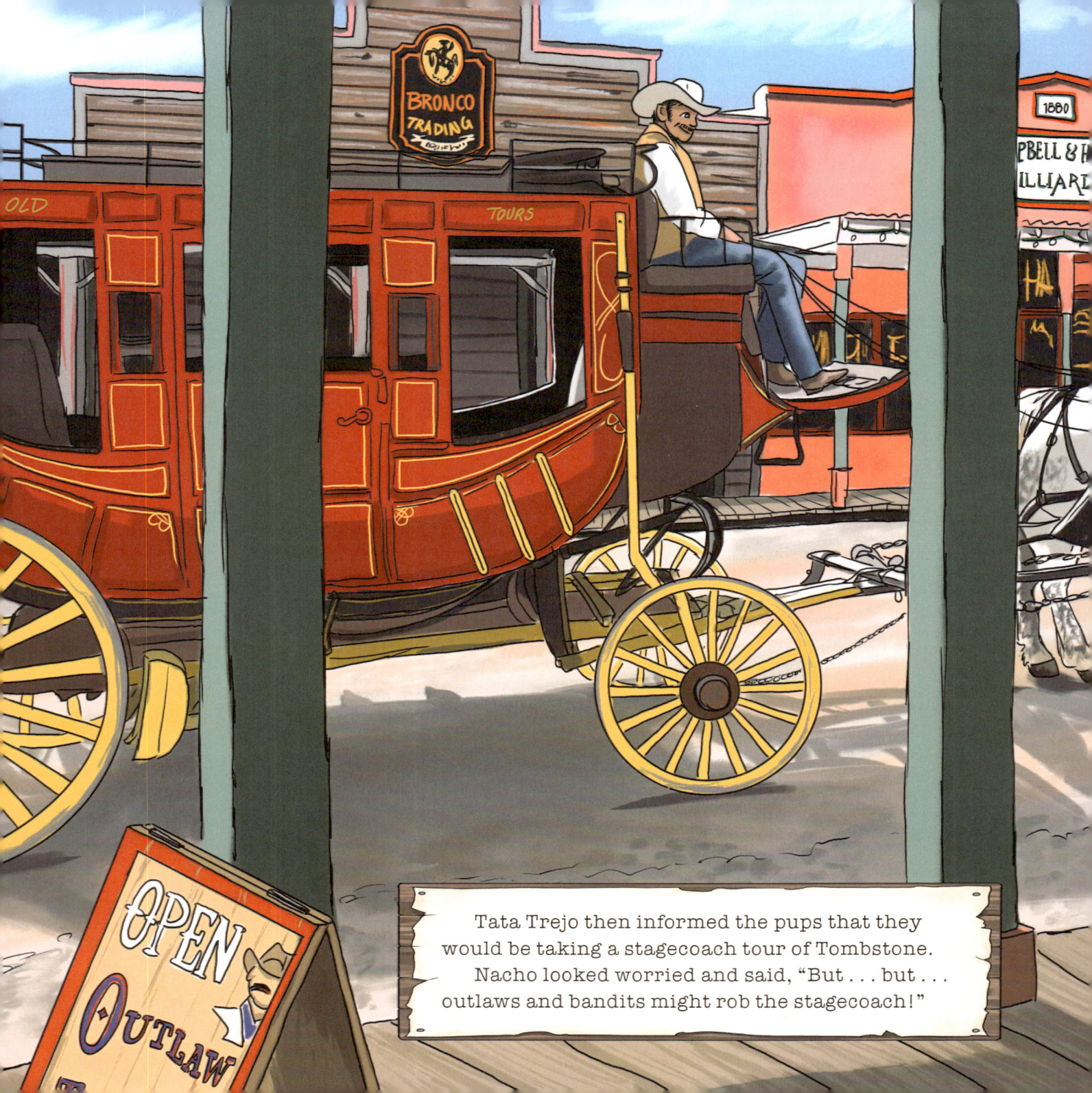

Tata Trejo then informed the pups that they would be taking a stagecoach tour of Tombstone. Nacho looked worried and said, "But . . . but . . . outlaws and bandits might rob the stagecoach!"

Lola chuckled and smiled. "No need to worry. We'll be just fine. We aren't carrying any silver or gold; we only have our dog treats. I don't think outlaws like dog treats."

The stagecoach made its first stop at Tombstone's historic jail and courthouse.

"What are those strange contraptions?" Nacho asked.

"Those are called jail cells and gallows," Lola said. "They're used to hold and punish outlaws. Let's get a photo."

"Ok. CHEESE!" Nacho grinned, posing for the photo.

Next, the stagecoach dropped the pups and Tata Trejo off at the town's printing shop.

When they got inside, Nacho pointed at something that looked like an old machine. "What are those big metal plates with letters engraved on them?" he asked.

The stagecoach tour continued through the town's dirt and rutted streets, passing historical buildings and landmarks, such as the Birdcage Theater, Big Nose Kate's saloon, and the Crystal Palace gambling hall.

As they reached the end of town, the stagecoach dropped them off at the Good Enough Silver Mine.

Lola handed Nacho a miner's cap and said, "We're heading underground to see what it was like to work in the silver mines back in the 1800s."

"Underground? Into the dark?" Nacho began to tremble. "I don't like the dark."

Lola gave him a reassuring pat on the head. "Yes, but no need to be scared. Our miner's hats have headlamps on them. You'll be able to see just fine."

"Okay, Lola. I trust you, and I can't wait to find silver and strike it rich!" Nacho said, pumping his paw in the air.

After the silver mine tour, they all headed back into town. Suddenly, they heard shouting and gunshots and saw the sheriff and his deputies in a gunfight. Bang! Bang! Bang!

"Duck for cover, Lola!" Nacho yelled, shaking with fear.

"No need to duck or worry, Nacho," Lola said. "This is the reenactment of the famous gunfight at the O.K. Corral."

"What's a reenactment, and why was it so famous?" Nacho asked.

"Well, Nacho, a reenactment means acting out a past event. The one they're doing today was a shootout between the sheriff, Wyatt Earp, his brothers, his friend Doc Holiday, and some outlaws called the Clanton-McLaury gang. The outlaws started the gunfight, and some people even died. The ones who died are buried in the town's famous cemetery."

"Yes, but Boothill is a very strange name for a cemetery," Nacho replied.
"It's called Boothill because many gunslingers died with their boots on."
Lola pointed to her cowboy boots.

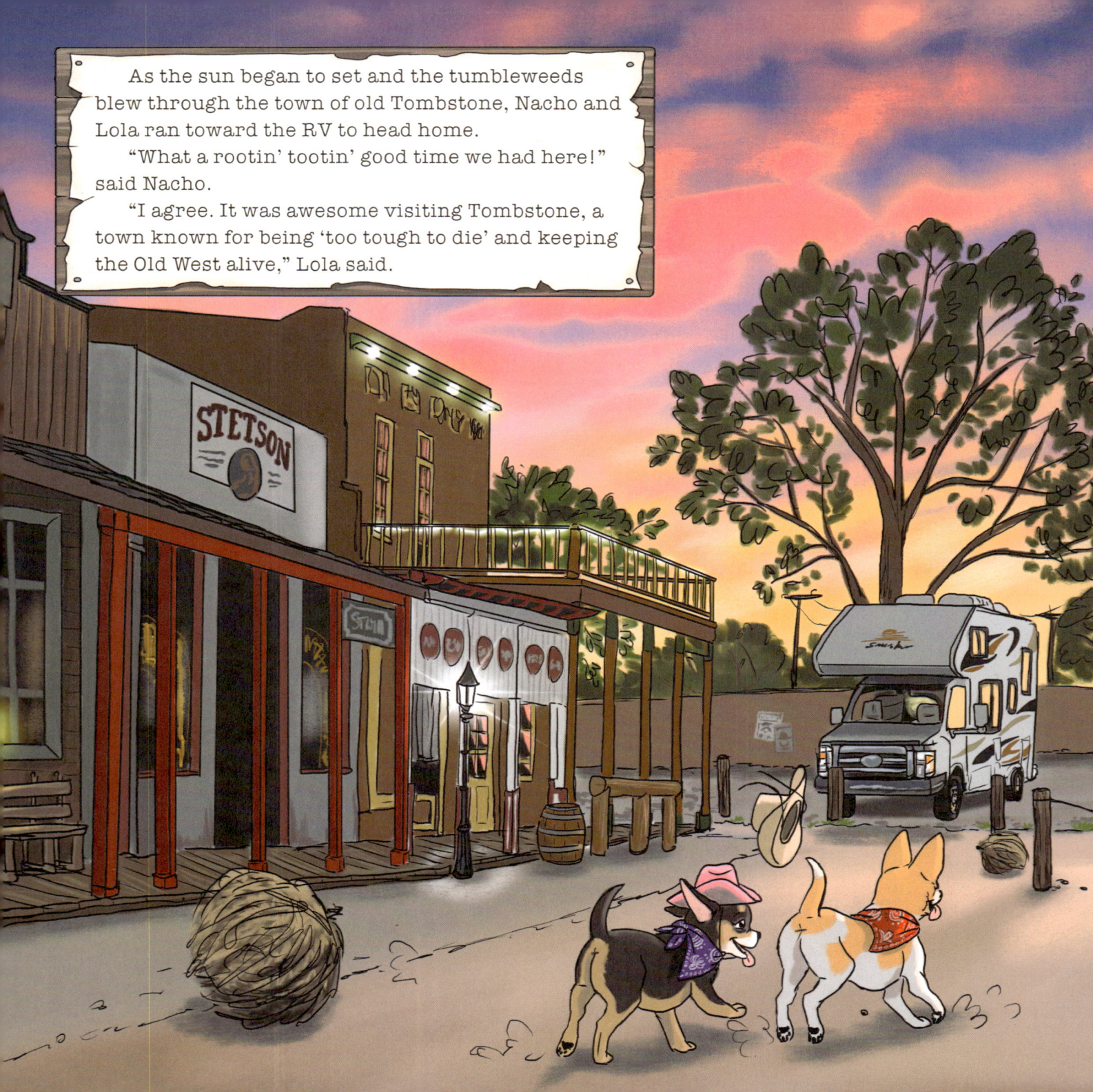

As the sun began to set and the tumbleweeds blew through the town of old Tombstone, Nacho and Lola ran toward the RV to head home.

"What a rootin' tootin' good time we had here!" said Nacho.

"I agree. It was awesome visiting Tombstone, a town known for being 'too tough to die' and keeping the Old West alive," Lola said.

Nacho and Lola threw their cowboy hats in the air, and both yapped, "Yippee-ki-ay!"

Then they climbed back into the RV and bid farewell to Tombstone and the Wild, Wild West as they drove off into the desert sunset.

Terrilyn is a retired special education teacher from Arizona who lives with her husband, Vidal. She loves spending time with her friends and family, especially her grandchildren! She enjoys reading, crafting, party planning, RV camping, and traveling. Terrilyn's desire to explore our beautifully diverse country (especially the desert Southwest) the wonderful memories of her beloved Chihuahuas, Nacho and Lola, and her passion for children's literature, led her to write these beloved children's books.

author.trejo2@gmail.com   @terrilynmtrejoauthor

Emily Brunner is a wildlife artist and children's book illustrator with a degree in Zoology. She currently lives in Los Angeles, California, with her husband and two cats. Emily has been creating "books" since she was five and has six published works so far. Her goal with her art is to both entertain and educate, to create detailed illustrations that make you want to come back and see or learn something new each time. feel free to follow her art journey.

www.barefootseeker.com   @barefoot_seeker_art

www.ingramcontent.com/pod-product-compliance
Lightning Source LLC
Chambersburg PA
CBRC090841120626
46551CB00008B/720